Angry

Julie Murray

Abdo
EMOTIONS
Kids

abdopublishing.com

Published by Abdo Kids, a division of ABDO, PO Box 398166, Minneapolis, Minnesota 55439.
Copyright © 2017 by Abdo Consulting Group, Inc. International copyrights reserved in all countries.
No part of this book may be reproduced in any form without written permission from the publisher.

Printed in the United States of America, North Mankato, Minnesota.

052016

092016

Photo Credits: Glow Images, iStock, Shutterstock

Production Contributors: Teddy Borth, Jennie Forsberg, Grace Hansen

Design Contributors: Christina Doffing, Candice Keimig, Dorothy Toth

Cataloging-in-Publication Data

Names: Murray, Julie, author.

Title: Angry / by Julie Murray.

Description: Minneapolis, MN : Abdo Kids, [2017] | Series: Emotions | Includes
    bibliographical references and index.

Identifiers: LCCN 2015959114 | ISBN 9781680805222 (lib. bdg.) |
    ISBN 9781680805789 (ebook) | ISBN 9781680806342 (Read-to-me ebook)

Subjects: LCSH: Anger--Juvenile literature. | Emotions--Juvenile literature.

Classification: DDC 152.5/7--dc23

LC record available at http://lccn.loc.gov/2015959114

Table of Contents

Angry

We feel **heated** when we are angry. It is an **emotion**.

Dan's team lost the game.

He feels angry.

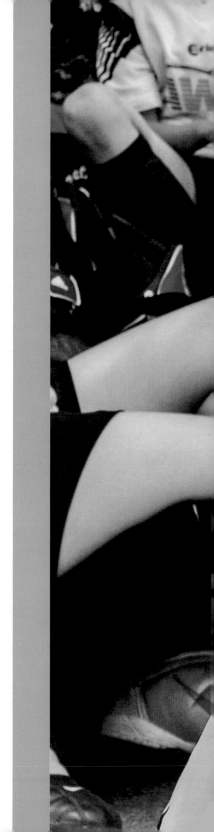

Another word for angry is mad.

9

Marco was pushed down.

He is angry.

Evan's sister took his book.

He is angry.

Bela dropped her ice cream.

She feels angry.

Sue wants to play. She has to finish her homework first. She gets angry.

John was left out of the game.

He is angry.

When have you felt angry?

21

Things to Do When We Are Angry

count to 30 or until
you feel calm

use words to say why
you are upset

play outside

walk away from what is
making you mad

Glossary

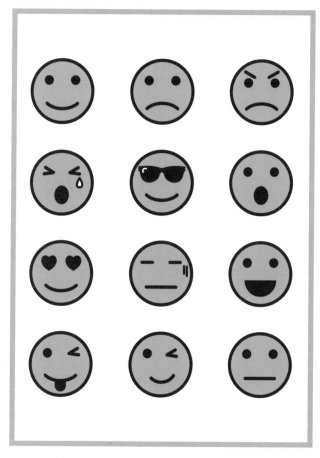

emotion
a strong feeling.

heated
marked by angry or excited feelings.

Index

abdokids.com

Use this code to log on to abdokids.com and access crafts, games, videos, and more!

Abdo Kids Code:
EAK5222